DONALD TRUMP

University Press
Copyright © 2016
All Rights Reserved

Table of Contents

Introduction
Chapter 1: Ancestry, Birth, and Childhood
Chapter 2: College and the Draft
Chapter 3: First Years in Real Estate
Chapter 4: Marriages, Children, and Divorces
Chapter 5: Ventures, Buildings, and Developments
Chapter 6: Bankruptcies
Chapter 7: Lawsuits and Investigations
Chapter 8: Other Financial Matters
Chapter 9: Entertainment
Chapter 10: Selling Entrepreneurship
Chapter 11: Religion
Chapter 12: Into Politics
Chapter 13: Positions on Domestic Affairs
Chapter 14: On Immigration and Foreign Policy
Chapter 15: Presidential Race 2016
Conclusion

Introduction

If only one word could be used to describe Donald Trump, it would have to be "big." He is tall and broad-shouldered. He has a fat bankroll and an extravagant lifestyle. He has a super-sized personality. Right now, he has a massive following. The man has become something of a legend in his own time.

Best known as a businessman and entertainer, Trump has also been interested in politics for many years. Yet, his political statements have often been overlooked - until now. Suddenly, the coverage of his speeches and activities has been unprecedented, and, like it or not, the world is listening.

Donald Trump has been a very public person for a long time, but who is the man behind the photo images splashed across social media and the sound bites played on the news every night? He seems unafraid of stating his opinion, no matter how politically incorrect it might seem. His opponents latch onto every coarse or inappropriate word he says in hopes of discrediting his legitimacy. At the same time, his avid supporters cheer whenever he speaks.

Despite allegations of unfair or unscrupulous business practices, Trump continues to be a force to be reckoned with, rolling along on his own enormous personal command of every situation. Few in the world have seized that power with such gusto.

People who wield such influence make both friends and enemies, and Trump is no exception. His friends congratulate him on his successes and his apparently honest portrayal of current political issues. Yet, his enemies have gone so far as to compare him to some of the most notorious tyrants in history.

Who is this man? Beginning with the story of his ancestry, birth, and childhood, discover where the Trump legend ends and the man begins.

Chapter 1

Ancestry, Birth, and Childhood

Donald Trump is a U.S. citizen, and his parents were U.S. citizens before he was born. His ancestors and all four of his grandparents, on the other hand, lived in Scotland or Germany. His paternal grandfather, Frederich Trump, came from Bavaria in 1885. After becoming a citizen, Frederick, a new name he had chosen for his new life, got rich in the Alaskan Gold Rush by providing gold seekers with dining and accommodations on their journeys.

Frederick's fortune went to his wife upon his death, and then to his son Fred, who used it to establish Elizabeth Trump and Sons, a business enterprise that is now known as the Trump Organization. Fred Trump made it big in New York real estate before fathering Donald Trump. Trump's mother, Mary Macleod, born in Scotland, emigrated to the U.S. at the age of 17 and became a maid in New York City. Fred married Mary in 1936, and Mary became a citizen in 1942. Fred was in the real estate business, building and managing apartments for middle-income renters.

On June 14, 1946, Fred and Mary Trump had a son, whom they named Donald John Trump. The family lived in an upscale neighborhood in Queens, and there were five children. Donald was the fourth. Due to Fred's inherited wealth and successful business, the family was very well off and lived lives of privilege and comfort.

Donald went to Kew-Forest School as a child. The school is a private college-prep school for children in preschool through high school. His father was a board member of the school. Donald was bright but unfortunately had behavior problems. So, before his eighth-grade year, his family sent him to New York Military Academy in hopes of straightening him out and teaching him discipline.

At the military academy, Donald was trained in military drills and leadership while taking the usual high school courses. When he arrived at the school, according to his former instructor Col. Ted Dobias, he was clueless about how to take care of himself the way cadets were required to do. He had to learn how to make a bed, shine his shoes, and most importantly, how to follow the rules laid down by the school.

Trump received no favoritism based on his parents' wealth and position, but he did well at the school and eventually proved himself sufficiently disciplined to attain the rank of Captain. Socially, he was a success at the school, bringing home girls from the upper levels of society frequently.

However, he never got close to his male classmates, who may have felt intimidated by him. He was very competitive, as he still is, and sometimes his air of superiority caused his classmates to dislike him. The school permitted hazing at that time. At one point in his senior year, Donald Trump allegedly hazed a freshman so mercilessly that Trump was transferred to a different student command.

Donald was always energetic as a teenager, working on his father's construction sites during the summers and playing sport during the school year. In 1964, with his secondary education behind him, Trump was ready to begin his higher education.

Chapter 2

College and The Draft

Donald Trump started at Fordham University in the fall of 1964. Little has been made public about Trump's two years at Fordham; however, some of the students do remember him as the guy who wore expensive clothes and had his own fancy car. Now, though, Matthew Santucci, editor of the *Fordham Political Review*, says that Trump does not acknowledge the school and the school does not acknowledge him, either.

Trump transferred to the Wharton School of Business and Commerce of the University of Pennsylvania in 1966. Trump has written that going to this school "doesn't prove very much," but also has said that it is impressive to the people he deals with in business circles. Possibly for this very reason, he mentions the school often during his presidential campaign.

There is some mystery surrounding Trump's performance at Wharton. While it was reported in the 1970s that Trump graduated at the top of his class, more recently, there have been questions. According to a report by *The New York Times*, Trump's name is not mentioned anywhere on the commencement program as someone who graduated with honors.

One writer, Jerome Tucccille, alleges that Trump only went to Wharton to make his father happy and that he did only what he had to in order to graduate while putting his real efforts into outside business deals. Several students who attended Wharton at the same time as Trump allege that he was not outstanding and not very involved with others at the university. Whether these allegations are true or not, Donald did graduate from Wharton in 1968.

Meanwhile, the Vietnam War was going on, and there was a draft. Donald applied for and received four deferments to attend school, as many men did at that time. After college, his classification changed to "available for service."

However, when he went in for his physical, he received a medical deferment. Trump has said the reason was that he had heel spurs. In late 1969, a new lottery system was started. The Selective Service issued Trump the number 356.

Since that number was never reached, he would not have served even if he had not had the medical deferment. He also never volunteered, and so did not serve in Vietnam.

Although Trump's experiences with the draft were not at all uncommon, they became an issue during his campaign for President of the United States. At a campaign event in 2015, Trump suggested that Senator John McCain, who was captured and then tortured for five years in Vietnam, was only a war hero because he became a prisoner of war, and that he liked those who managed to escape that fate.

When asked if he would apologize to McCain, Trump explained that it was wrong that the people who fought and did not get captured got no recognition, so no, he would not apologize. Nevertheless, no evidence has been shown that Trump was a draft dodger in any commonly-used sense of the word. He further said that if he had been drafted, he would have "proudly served."

However, since he was not in Vietnam, he had time to devote to business in the U.S. He began making real estate deals when he was in college and joined his father in the Trump Organization.

The next years would be a whirlwind of activity for him and would afford him many opportunities to display his business acumen.

Chapter 3

First Years in Real Estate

Donald Trump's first foray into real estate came during his college years when he worked for his father's company, Elizabeth Trump and Son. The company's primary business concern was buying, managing, and selling middle-income housing. While the company mainly conducted business in New York City, Donald's first opportunity came in an apartment complex in Cincinnati, Ohio. He joined the company in 1968.

Trump's father had already bought the Swifton Village apartments for $5.7 million two years before Donald entered college. When Donald got involved, he convinced his father to use equity loans to expand the company. His father eventually agreed and put $500,000 into renovating the complex. The pair turned a sparsely-populated complex into a successful one with 100% occupancy. They sold it for $6.75 in 1972. Meanwhile, they were raking in profits.

By the time Trump graduated, he had amassed what would now be equivalent to over $1 million.

Donald moved to Manhattan in 1971, where he lived in a studio apartment. While there, he became head of Elizabeth Trump and Son. Before long, he changed the name of the company to the Trump Organization. He collaborated on several major construction projects. The buildings were designed to stand out as some of the most attractive buildings in the area. These were popular sites and helped Donald achieve more recognition than he had previously enjoyed.

As Trump Organization president, Trump was responsible for 14,000 apartments in Queens, Staten Island, and Brooklyn. Trump acquired an option on the Pennsylvania Central Railroad's rail yards after that company entered bankruptcy. In 1978, he suggested to the mayor of New York that the site would be perfect for a convention center. He won the bid on the job, being the only builder who had a suitable site immediately available. Because he brokered the deal, he received a generous payment.

Trump went on to bigger things that same year when he built the Grand Hyatt Hotel. He was able to get many investors in the project after convincing the city to give a 40-year tax abatement on the hotel in exchange for a percentage of the profits. Donald's father Fred was a silent partner and helped Donald get the deal through his association with an Equitable officer.

In an incredible 1981 deal, Trump negotiated a rental agreement on a building on Fifth Avenue in Midtown Manhattan next to Tiffany & Company. During the demolition of the building, several Art Deco sculptures were destroyed, sparking controversy. However, construction still moved ahead. By the time he was finished renovating the building and adding to it, it became Trump Tower, which is an opulent building, with a 60-foot waterfall and a 5-level atrium. Trump Tower became the center point of the Trump Organization. The Trump Organization's creations have been nothing short of magnificent when they were constructed, and many of them remain as awe-inspiring visions of cutting-edge architecture.

During this time, he also began his first family after marrying in 1977. The marriage would last long enough to produce three children and garner his wife a hefty divorce settlement.

Chapter 4

Marriages, Children and Divorces

In 1976, Ivana Zeinickova, who had arrived in Canada from Czechoslovakia several years earlier, went to New York on a modeling job. There, she met Donald Trump. After a whirlwind romance, the two married in 1977. This was Donald's first marriage, but Ivana's second. Trump put Ivana in charge of interior design on many of his major projects.

Donald and Ivana were stars among the elite in New York social circles during the 80s. Their first son, Donald Trump, Jr., was born on December 31, 1977. Two years later, on October 30, 1981, their daughter Ivanka Trump was born. They had a third child, Eric Trump, who was born on January 6, 1984.

All three children from Donald and Ivana's marriage have become successful in business. Donald Trump, Jr., a father of five, has been married to wife Vanessa since 2005. He loves hunting and fishing and became very close with his Czech grandfather Milos, who enjoyed the same activities until his death in 1990. Donald Jr. worked for his father for minimum wage when he was a teenager but now draws a substantial income as an executive vice president of the Trump Organization.

Donald and Ivana's daughter Ivanka was a model for a short time before getting into real estate and then joining the Trump Organization to become an executive vice president. She also has her own fashion and jewelry lines. Ivanka is married and has three children. She often takes the position of lead negotiator on Trump business deals.

The third child Donald and Ivanka had together is Eric. Eric went to Georgetown University and then immediately joined the Trump Organization as executive vice president. He owns Trump Wintery and donates millions to the St. Jude Research Hospital through his charitable foundation. He is married to Lara.

Up until 1988, Ivana was still a Czech citizen. Donald Trump accompanied her to a ceremony that year as she became a U.S. citizen.

However, their marriage, which had always been volatile, became even more hostile when Donald began having an affair with another model, Marla Maples. When Donald and Ivana divorced in 1991, Ivana received a $20 million settlement even though the Trump Organization was in bankruptcy. Ivana agreed as a part of the divorce settlement not to discuss her relationship with The Donald, as she called him, but she broke the gag clause when she wrote a tell-all book about him.

After the divorce, Donald spent his off-time with his girlfriend, Marla. When the two had a child on October 13, 1993, whom they named Tiffany, Donald and Marla decided to marry and tied the knot on December 20 that same year. They separated less than four years later, and their divorce concluded in June, 1999.

Tiffany, unlike Ivana's children, has gone her own direction, going into music and working at Vogue. She enjoys traveling and often uses a Trump private jet to visit foreign cities.

Donald's third and present wife is Melania Trump. Born Melania Knauss in Slovenia, Melania has since obtained citizenship in the

U.S. The two became a couple in 1998 and married on January 22, 2005.

Their son, Barron William Trump, was born on March 20, 2006. While Melania has kept Barron's life largely private, she has taken him to child social events and to the Trump International Grand Prix. He has lived an extravagant lifestyle. At one interview, Melanie described using a caviar-based moisturizer on him after every bath. A bright child, he enjoys building and golf.

Although Trump has been something of a serial monogamist, it seems that his first love has always been his business. Although he has had business failures along with business success, he has never turned away from it. So, as the marriages came and went, he continued to buy, build, and sell real estate along with other business ventures.

Chapter 5

Ventures, Buildings, and Developments

When casinos were approved in Atlantic City in 1977, Trump began gathering facts about the gambling business. He acquired a property in that city in 1980 for that purpose, and Holiday Inn joined him in the venture in 1982. Trump developed the site, and it opened in 1984 under the name Harrah's at Trump Plaza.

True to form, Trump went big with the project, including a complex with 614 rooms and a 60,000 square foot casino. Trump bought out Harrah's two years after the complex opened. He purchased neighboring hotels, expanding the Trump Plaza Hotel and Casino further in 1993. In 2011, Trump decided to expand it again, but he could not reach an agreement with the lender to acquire the funds to do it. It officially closed in September 2014.

Trump scooped up the Taj Mahal before its developers had completed it, in 1990. At that time, it was the largest hotel-casino in the world, and it is still among the top 50.

At about that time, Trump decided to purchase a site facing Central Park in New York and build a large condominium tower. However, an apartment building stood on the site, and its residents fought the move. Since the apartments were rent-controlled under the rent stabilization program, the tenants won out.

At the same time, Trump bought the Barbizon-Plaza Hotel, renovated it, and renamed it Trump Parc. He bought 76 acres of land in west Manhattan to build a complex he would call Television City, intending to put twelve skyscrapers, a park and a mall on the site. Television City was slated to have the world's tallest building. When opposition in the community and a slow city approval time delayed the project, Trump abandoned the idea. He also purchased the Plaza Hotel, and his then-wife Ivana managed its renovation.

However, in the early 1990s, Trump's ventures began to flounder financially. From 1991 to 2009, he declared bankruptcy four times.

Although he has never declared personal bankruptcy, he used the laws in an effort to stay in business and keep amassing wealth. The Trump Organization survived, but Donald Trump's wealth declined from $1.7 billion to $500 million. Trump was not down for long, though, and by 1997, his net worth grew to $2 billion.

Trump continued to add to his acquisitions and projects, buying up hotels, estates, and complexes to renovate or construct his extravagant buildings. He bought an estate called Mar-a-Lago and turned it into a winter residence and an exclusive private club for the rich and famous. He constructed Trump Place in 2002. The Hotel Delmonico became Trump Park Avenue luxury condominiums in 2004.

Since then, Trump has built his business up further, adding several golf course resorts, products like bottled water called Trump Ice, publications such as Trump Books and Trump Magazine, and a variety of eateries and bars. Trump has also licensed his likeness and name, which other businesses use by paying for the privilege, providing Trump with one of many sources of residual income. Yet, with all this success, those bankruptcies continue to be a source of criticism from the public.

Chapter 6

Bankruptcies

Trump has used Chapter 11 bankruptcy laws to decrease debts on his businesses. Trump's seemingly casual use of bankruptcy has been the subject of minor public criticism on and off for many years. After he declared his candidacy for president in the 2016 election, the controversy resurfaced and grew. Trump has pointed to this practice as a tool many great entrepreneurs use.

Trump's first bankruptcy was filed in 1991 to rescue the debt-ridden Taj Mahal. After having financed the project with junk bonds despite telling the New Jersey Casino Control Commission that he would not do that, the high-interest debt became a problem. Trump went public with the casino, selling 50% of the company in stocks and bonds to cover the debt in a "prepackaged bankruptcy."

Next to declare bankruptcy the following year was Trump Plaza. According to Trump Plaza executive John "Jack" O'Donnell, Trump panicked about the plaza's future after several Trump Taj Mahal executives were killed in a helicopter accident in 1989. O'Donnell also alleges that all the profits from the casino were continually being taken out to service other debts. By 1992, Trump Plaza was failing. *The Washington Post* alleges that Trump used the deaths of the Taj Mahal executives to excuse the failures in Atlantic City.

In 1994, Trump sold several items to raise funds, including his Trump Shuttle airline and Trump Princess yacht. This not only decreased his personal debt but also reduced his $3.5 billion business debt. However, he still had Trump Tower and control of three casinos.

The third bankruptcy happened in 2004. Trump's three Atlantic City hotel/casinos and others made up the Trump Hotels & Casino Resorts. That business, too, floundered. Trump had 56% ownership before the bankruptcy but had to give up half that as well as his position as CEO. He was still chairman of the board. The company came back out of bankruptcy renamed Trump Entertainment Resorts Holdings. In 2007, Trump wrote that he told the banker it was a mistake to loan Trump the money in the first place, and that "the deal was no good."

Technically, Trump was not the one who filed bankruptcy the fourth time, although the timing of his and Ivanka's departure from the board of Trump Entertainment Resorts was only four days before the 2009 bankruptcy happened. Trump had sued the casino and took away $100 million from that action in the bankruptcy. Trump then negotiated to reduce the debt owed to the bondholders by $1 billion.

Although many in public see these bankruptcies as negative aspects of Trump's business dealings, Trump and many of his supporters maintain that this is a routine part of the business for high-powered entrepreneurs. However, over the years, other troubling allegations about Donald's business practices have marred the Trump name in some circles.

Chapter 7

Lawsuits and Investigations

Donald Trump, like many corporate leaders, has had his share of troubles. Legal issues and investigations have been an ongoing part of the Trump Organization's business. According to *USA TODAY*, hundreds of people have alleged that Trump did not pay them or only paid them partially or late. Allegations of unfair or discriminatory business practices have also surfaced over the years.

In 1973, the Justice Department investigated Fred and Donald Trump due to allegations that they were refusing to rent to blacks. After lengthy negotiations, the federal government agreed to allow the Trumps to say they had done nothing wrong. The Trumps' responsibility in the deal was to accept blacks and other minorities who were pre-screened and sent to them by the Urban League. The Justice Department later said that Trump's racial discrimination was so persistent that it became an obstacle to equal opportunity. Later though, the New York Human Rights Commission's chairperson said the reason the Trumps were singled out in this lawsuit was because of their recognizable names.

In 1983, when Trump demolished the Bonwit Teller store to create space for Trump Tower, the contractor allegedly used 200 undocumented immigrant workers and paid them only $4 to $5 per hour for working 12-hour shifts. The matter went to court, and in 1990 Trump testified that he knew nothing about the issue, as he was rarely at that location. The court records were eventually sealed in 1999 when the issue was finally settled.

A business analyst who had said the Taj Mahal project would fail within a year sued Trump for defamation in 1990. Trump had told the analyst's firm that he would sue them unless they fired the analyst, and the analyst was fired. Trump and the analyst settled the case. The Taj Mahal went into bankruptcy in 1990.

In 1991, Trump sued the maker of the helicopter in which his executives were killed in 1989. He lost the suit.

In 1997, Jill Harth Houraney, sued Trump for $125 million because he allegedly sexually harassed her for many years beginning with their first meeting. Trump denied and continues to deny anything like that ever happened. Houraney has never backed down on her story, but she did confirm that she attended one of his rallies for the 2016 presidential race and had thanked him for helping her.

The New York State Lobbying Commission fined Trump in 2000 for going around state law to lobby against the approval of an Indian casino, which might have taken business away from his Atlantic City casinos. Trump paid $250,000 to settle the fines.

Trump filed suit against the city of Rancho Palos Verdes, California in 2008, asking for $100 million. Trump alleged the city defrauded him and violated his civil rights. The city had put up resistance against Trump's building a housing development on a golf course that was allegedly prone to mudslides. Trump withdrew the suit in 2012 after he and the city agreed to modified geological surveys. The city extended permits for 20 additional homes and a conservation easement was established rather than expanding the housing development further.

Trump even sued a law firm he had previously hired, demanding $5 million when Morrison Cohen used his names and links to news articles related to Trump. This suit was dismissed.

Another lawsuit, in 2009, involved individuals who had paid deposits for condos in Trump Ocean Resort in Baja, Mexico. The construction of condos there were canceled, and the investors sued Trump when he did not return their money. Trump claimed he had been only a spokesman and not in charge of the operation. The investors alleged he had misrepresented the situation. Trump settled with the condo owners.

The planned but never completed Trump International Hotel & Tower in Fort Lauderdale Beach was the subject of over ten lawsuits starting in 2009. Five years earlier, the project had started, but by 2009, the real estate market had declined, and Trump ended his licensing deal with his partner. After the project defaulted on a $139 million loan, investors sued for fraud. Trump demanded his name be taken off the building, but his petition was denied because he had been involved with marketing the project.

Many other suits were filed by and against Trump during these years. According to *USA TODAY*, at least 60 lawsuits concerning employees and contractors that Trump allegedly failed to pay have been filed, and at least 253 subcontractors were not paid as much or as soon as promised. And, new lawsuits have been brought after 2010.

Trump sued Scotland in 2011. He alleged it built the Aberdeen Bay Wind Farm where they had assured him they would not build. With the wind farm in place, Trump lost his chosen location to build a hotel next to his golf course. The Supreme Court of the United Kingdom denied his suit in a unanimous vote in 2015.

Trump has indeed gone big with his life, and that includes the kinds of lawsuits he has filed. Then, too, when someone exerts that much financial power, they are naturally going to have opponents. So, he has also been on the receiving end of lawsuits throughout the years.

The finances of Donald Trump and the Trump Organization have always been complex, as is true of any major corporation, especially one headed by a bold entrepreneur. Other issues and allegations have come up over the years, including tax disputes, allegations of dealing with some unsavory characters, and the question of Donald Trump's net worth.

Chapter 8

Other Financial Matters

When Donald Trump became the Republican nominee for president in 2016, several individuals questioned whether Trump was as wealthy as he claimed to be. And, as is usual for presidential candidates, Trump had to deal with questions about his tax returns. Perhaps less common, people wondered about rumors that Trump allegedly associated with members of organized crime.

Trump had sued Timothy L. O'Brien, the author of an unauthorized biography, *TrumpNation: The Art of Being the Donald*. O'Brien had reported that Trump was worth no more than $250 million, but Trump said that allegation is false and that he is worth billions. In 2011, an appellate court ruled against Trump's suit, saying that O'Brien's confidential sources were consistent.

The question arose again during Trump's 2016 campaign, as Mitt Romney and others alleged that he was hiding the answer by not disclosing his tax returns. Trump denied their allegations, saying that an audit was going on that precluded him from disclosing the returns. This is a common and legal practice for people who are being audited.

According to Trump, the return in question is being audited along with all returns since 2009. He said that he would reveal the content of the returns before the November 2016 presidential election if the audits were completed by then. He also alleged that the government was being unfair to him by auditing him so many years in a row.

Despite all the controversy over Trump's net worth, *Forbes* and *Bloomberg* have both estimated his net worth at over $3 billion. Yet, the issue seems far from settled. Federal election regulators reported that his assets were worth $1.4 billion, but Trump produced an accounting firm's report saying he was worth over $8 billion.

In a 2015 campaign press release, Trump was said to be worth over $10 million. About the FEC filing that reported his gross revenue as over $611 million for that year, the release said that the type of filing required was not designed for someone with Trump's "massive wealth" and that his net worth frequently fluctuates with the market and changes in attitude.

Journalists Wayne Barrett and David Cay Johnston allege that Trump has done business with members of the mafia. However, there has been no serious allegation that Trump did anything illegal with or for them. Also relevant is the fact that people who were around at the time suggest that working with mafia members was a standard part of the business then.

Trump has gone for the big and bold in many ways, and his financial issues are at the heart of his brand. Yet, not all of his investments have worked out. One area with both pluses and minuses for Trump has been the entertainment industry. His entertainment ventures have sometimes failed. At other times, they have succeeded beyond all expectations, except for perhaps Trump's own.

Chapter 9

Entertainment

In 2006, when Donald Trump was working with Fran and Barry Weissler to produce a musical based on his TV reality show *The Apprentice*, Weissler said that the stage might be the only medium sufficient to showcase Trump's "larger than life" personality. The show never went forward. Still, considering the phenomenal success of *The Apprentice*, it is hard to imagine it would have been anything other than profitable.

Trump began his efforts to produce a smash hit back when he was just 23 years old. He went to Broadway producer David Black with an interest in becoming a producer on Black's play "Paris is Out!," along with $70,000 to back up his ambition. Trump had apparently gathered information about the theater business before the meeting. Black agreed to give him equal billing, and the deal was on.

Trump already had a flair for business and used it to market the play. However, the play flopped, losing both Black's and Trump's investments. If Trump was discouraged, it was only for a time. He came back to the entertainment business with even grander ideas later on.

In 1999, Donald founded Trump Model Management. The company has found some of the most beautiful women in the world and managed their modeling careers. Another venture has been ice skating rinks, where one can take skating classes, hone hockey skills, or even have a birthday party with 2,000 friends.

Trump's *The Apprentice* showed up on television in January 2004. Audiences were thrilled with Donald's flair for the dramatic as job seekers vied to impress Trump with their business management skills in a variety of business-oriented tasks.

Ratings skyrocketed, and the show was an instant and outstanding success. Trump's children were introduced to the general public as they joined their father as advisors. The show also had critical success, receiving three Emmy's during its 14 seasons.

In *The Celebrity Apprentice*, Trump used a similar format, but the goal for the celebrities was to raise money for charities and win the privilege of spending the next year doing the same under the supervision of the Trump Organization. In addition to the two Apprentice shows, Trump Productions, LLC is the force behind the "Miss USA Pageant."

The news about the pageant was not always favorable to Trump. While the lavish production pleased many pageant enthusiasts, one of the contestants was so opposed to Trump Productions' handling of the 2012 pageant that she took her outrage to social media. Miss Pennsylvania, Sheena Monnin, alleged that the pageants had been fixed before the competition took place.

Donald seemed to understand the significance of the pageant for Americans as well as the profitability potential for himself. He spoke out against Monnin's accusations and eventually sued her for $5 million. She lost the suit, but said on Inside Edition that she never had to pay anything "out of pocket." Trump sold his interests in the Miss USA, Miss Universe, and Miss Teen Universe in 2015.

In 2013, Trump sued Bill Maher, who had said on *The Tonight Show with Jay Leno* that if Trump could produce a birth certificate showing he was not the son of his mother and an orangutan, Maher would pay $5 million. Trump took Maher's words seriously, produced the document, and demanded to be paid. When Maher would not give him the money, he filed suit against him. However, he dropped the suit a few weeks later.

Trump Productions continues to come up with popular shows, both for network TV and cable. The long and short of it is that many TV viewers are in love with Trump's style. And, calling on that same winning persona and distinct brand, Trump has also intrigued many individuals who want to have the same type of success as entrepreneurs as Donald has enjoyed.

Chapter 10

Selling Entrepreneurship

As with many of Trump's ventures, his publications, products, and classes have been met with both praise and scorn. One thing is certain: Donald Trump believes in entrepreneurship.

Trump's books have been wildly popular, both among budding entrepreneurs and among people who enjoy reading the inside story of success directly from this fascinating man who has achieved it in so many ways. As of this writing, Amazon lists 43 books by Trump.

Trump: The Art of the Deal lists Donald Trump and Tony Schwartz as its authors. Trump spent many hours with Schwartz during an 18-month period beginning in 1985, talking about his life and business, and Schwartz wrote the book. In 2015, as Trump began his quest for the White House, he told an audience that America needed "the leader who wrote *The Art of the Deal*." And, although Trump was not the one who actually wrote the book, he was undoubtedly the one behind many of the ideas and conversations in it.

Trump has also made several financial deals involving sports. In 1983, he bought a football team that would play in the new United States Football League. Donald sold the team and then repurchased it before the second season started. The league folded in 1986. Trump hosted boxing events at Trump Plaza in Atlantic City. For at least one of Mike Tyson's bouts, Trump was his advisor on the financial aspects of the fight. In addition, he has held two WrestleMania events at Trump Plaza and participated in those and other WWE events. He was inducted into the WWE Hall of Fame, celebrity wing, in 2013.

Starting in 2015, Donald Trump offered education to others who wanted to follow in his footsteps through his Trump Wealth Institute, which became Trump University and then Trump Entrepreneur Initiative, offered classes in entrepreneurship and real estate at the price of up to $35,000 per class.

In 2013, Trump University came under fire. The New York Attorney General Eric Schneiderman filed suit against Trump, alleging that the defrauded over 5,000 people of $40 million. This money was allegedly gained illegally by Trump because he used the term "university" to entice individuals to pay for lessons in Trump's investment techniques. Trump countersued, alleging that the attorney general's investigation had been tied to campaign funding requests. The counterclaim was dismissed in 2015.

A class-action suit was also brought against Trump by former students in the matter. One of these students, Marla Makaeff, allegedly continued to take classes at Trump University after joining the class action suit and posted videos of the seminars on social media. Trump filed suit against her, but in 2015, a district judge ordered Trump to pay Makaeff and her lawyers for their legal fees.

That class-action suit, as well as another, is still ongoing as of this writing. Trump spoke out against one judge, whom he alleged could not be impartial because of his ethnicity and Trump's declaration that the U.S. should build a wall on its Mexican border. The statement drew criticism from people who alleged that he was a racist. That allegation would be repeated by his opponents over and over during his presidential campaign in 2016, but Trump's political aspirations began much earlier, and by the 1980s, he was already considering the top government job in America.

Still, GOP leaders tend to favor people who follow a religion, especially some form of Christianity. And, while Trump was not an overtly Christian leader, the facts show that he grew up with religion and has considered it an important issue throughout his life.

The religious views Trump has expressed helped define him in the eyes of both his supporters and detractors. As a candidate for President of the United States, these statements and actions could become important in determining his success or failure. Or, maybe not. Perhaps Donald Trump is so different from other candidates that they will not matter in the race at all. Still, many voters find them worth considering.

Chapter 11

Religion

Donald Trump made religion an issue in the 2016 presidential race by attacking the faith of others. Religion can be a touchy issue for many Americans, but Trump seems to have no trouble expressing his views on the subject. He does not seem to worry that others will not accept his views or that they will hurt his chances of becoming president. But then, Trump seems to have no problem stating his opinion on any issue.

As a boy, Donald began going to the Presbyterian Church – specifically, he and his parents and siblings went to the Marble Collegiate Church. Located in Manhattan, the church was a place where people went on Sundays to listen to Reverend Norman Vincent Peale speak on positivity and personal power for self-fulfillment. He was confirmed at that church and later on, married his first wife there.

As a presidential candidate in 2011, Trump told audiences that his "religion is a wonderful religion," and that he was a Presbyterian and a Protestant. Although Trump said later that he was not active in the church, he did express that he thought of Marble Collegiate as his home church.

Trump's daughter married a Jewish man and converted to his religion, giving Donald Trump Jewish grandchildren. He has indicated that this is not a problem for him and, in fact, he is happy about it.

Early in 2016, Pope Francis criticized Trump's stance on closing the Mexican border. The Pope explained that people who want to build walls are not Christian. Trump was outraged at this judgment of his religious faith. Many in the Christian community agreed, saying that no one else has the right or the ability to determine if someone is truly a Christian or not. Fair enough.

However, Trump's criticism of the Pope continued, angering many devout Catholics. At the same time, conservative Christians have supported Trump's comments. Trump has stated his opinion that what matters most is that the borders must be secured and that that is what people were responding to most when they chose to support him on this issue.

Eventually, the Pope's spokesman stated that the Pope was not going to interfere in the U.S. presidential race, nor had he said anything as harsh as the media had reported. Trump backed off from his criticism of the Pope, agreeing that the media had probably overstated the Pope's message as the story broke.

Further along in the campaign, after Donald was named as the Republican nominee, Trump told voters that no one knew about what kind of religious background and views his Democratic opponent, Hillary Clinton, espoused.

Later, reports surfaced that Trump had had a born-again religious experience. *Focus on the Family* founder Dr. James Dobson said Trump was a "baby Christian.". However, up to the time of this writing, Donald has not verified that this is so.

While Trump has said that he enjoys collecting copies of his favorite book – the Bible – and that he values his religion, many voters continued to wonder if it was all a ruse designed to get more votes. Still, most Christians are taught to be compassionate to others and not to judge by appearances. For this reason, along with other issues dear to the religious right, Trump may indeed carry the most conservative religious states.

Donald Trump's religious views may be questionable, at least for some Christians, but his positions on other significant issues are clear. Trump seems to know what he wants for the world in general and for America in particular. Most of all, he wants to "Make America Great Again." How will he do it?

Chapter 12

Into Politics

It is hard to say precisely when Donald Trump began thinking of being a politician. For all the general public knows, he might have dreamed of being president as a boy. Whenever his interest began, it came to public attention during the 1980s.

In 1988, George H.W. Bush and Michael Dukakis were the front-runners in the presidential race, with Jesse Jackson also a popular choice. Trump considered, on some level, whether to run for president at that time, and several influential people undoubtedly asked him whether he would run.

On The Oprah Winfrey Show that year, Oprah asked him if he would ever go for the presidency. Trump did not immediately say yes. However, during the interview, he explained that he might do it if things became worse in the U.S. government.

Trump predicted that he would win if he decided to run. He also spoke on the need to end illegal immigration and stop making free trade agreements. Trump was considered as a running mate for George H.W. Bush, but he later dropped out of the race. He did win the Republican Party's Michigan and California primaries, but it was after he withdrew his candidacy.

Trump briefly considered running again for the 2000 race but decided against it again. In 2004, he seemed to consider the top job more seriously than he had before. At that time, he was considering running as a Reform Party candidate. Again, he chose not to run.

In 2006, Trump's political future seemed to take a different tack. Trump was approached by several of the Republican leaders of New York to ask him to run for governor. He decided against it, saying that he was enjoying life in the real estate and building industry. One more thing: he said he might run for president in 2008. He did not appear to consider that seriously in 2007, but he was still interested in politics.

Many voters supported Trump's bid for the presidency in 2011. Even as he considered running, polls showed him even with or ahead of the other presidential candidates. He spoke out against President Obama, saying that Obama had not been born in the United States and so was not eligible to be president. He also criticized every possible candidate. He was winning in the polls among Republican voters.

However, President Obama did two things to increase his own popularity. He produced his birth certificate, and he announced that Osama bin Laden had been killed. Obama's popularity jumped then, and Trump's declined. At one point, a poll by CNN and the Opinion Research Corp. predicted that Trump would lose to Barack Obama by 22 points.

The Apprentice was still a popular show that year, but NBC executives reassured viewers that the show would go on in Trump's absence with another boss at the helm. They added that they supported Trump in his run for the presidency. However, it was not to be. Again, Trump bowed out before the Republican nominee was chosen. Trump told his supporters that he would continue to be a force in national politics.

The year 2013 saw another suggestion that Trump might eventually become president. Republican leaders, disgusted with what they saw as political corruption in New York, wanted him to run to unseat Governor Cuomo. Trump held many meetings with various GOP leaders, who told him that becoming a governor, especially in New York, would be the crucial step towards running for president in the next election.

When Trump let them know he would not run if they did not eliminate another candidate from the race, the party bigwigs told him they had no control over whether another candidate ran or not. They continued to insist that Trump needed to hold a high political position before running for president. Trump was not convinced that standard political moves were right for him. Yet again, Trump decided not to run and suggested that he never really considered it seriously. After all, what he really wanted was the White House.

Chapter 13

Positions on Domestic Affairs

Ever since Donald Trump entered the public eye, he has expressed opinions on the political issues of the day. And, after he declared his candidacy and then received the Republican nomination for President, his political opinions became more critical than they had before. At that point, they were no longer personal beliefs. They were ideas and attitudes that could shape the future of the United States. Trump's opinions on domestic affairs offer fresh perspectives on both old and new issues.

Years before becoming the Republican nominee for President, Trump had more liberal views. He called himself pro-choice and supported gay rights to a certain extent. However, Trump has admittedly "evolved" in his stance on abortion, partly because he says he knew someone who was going to have an abortion but did not, allowing a child to be born and live a wonderful life.

While Trump has said that the Planned Parenthood organization does help women, he has said that it should be defunded because of the abortions done there. He does say that abortions in the cases of rape, incest, and saving the mother's life should be allowed.

As of early August 2015, Trump had not taken positions on many of the other women's and family's issues. He gave no definitive stances on equal pay but did suggest that women who do the same jobs as men should (and probably do) get the same pay as men in the same positions if they do a good job.

Trump had not explicitly said whether or not he supported paid family leave, but did say that it was something "you have to be careful of." He indicated that he thought childcare could be done inexpensively by a company rather than by the government. Also, as of 2016, Trump opposed same-sex marriage and said it should be a state issue rather than a federal one.

Civil rights have not been a particularly strong central focus of Trump's views. Some members of the media have alleged that Trump is a racist and a misogynist. Trump denies these allegations are true, even though he has often been critical of minorities and women.

During a time of racial unrest centered around the police, Trump suggested that, although black lives do matter, having a strong police force is crucial. Furthermore, he talked at several times on the needs of police officers to have better treatment and more respect in the community.

As for gun control, Donald Trump opposes it strongly. Rather than limit the Second Amendment rights of all people, he proposes working to improve the federal background check system to ensure criminals and mentally ill people do not get guns.

It is not exactly a surprise to most people that Trump favored cutting taxes for corporations. He also, however, proposed closing the loopholes and ending many business deductions. He said he wanted to lower personal taxes in general. He supported eliminating the estate tax that was at that time in place for estates over $5.45 million.

Trump places himself in the free-trade camp but opposes NAFTA and the World Trade Organization. He supports making trade fairer for America by increasing or adding tariffs, especially on exports to the U.S. coming from China and Mexico. He said on several occasions that the U.S. does not beat China, Japan, and Mexico on trade.

Trump spoke out vehemently against "Obamacare," saying the Affordable Care Act should be thrown out and replaced with a different type of free-market system. He supports giving individuals the ability to claim deductions for health care premiums. He also said Medicare should be controlled by the states rather than the federal government.

In education, Trump opposed the Common Core Curriculum, a position that resonated with many parents in the U.S. He supported school choice and favors giving primary and secondary schools local control. He favors getting rid of the Department of Education.

On environmental issues, Trump's words rang true for those who do not accept the scientific community's assessment of climate change. He called global warming a hoax and expressed his view that the U.S. should back out of the Paris Climate Agreement because it treats China and other countries more favorably than the U.S.

Donald Trump's ideas on domestic issues are unique, and his opinions on foreign policy and immigration are also quite distinctive. With the election still two months ahead, Trump had flip-flopped back and forth on some of these issues while remaining steady on others.

Chapter 14

On Immigration and Foreign Policy

The general public sometimes saw Donald Trump as a person who was very intense when it came to immigration. But then, the 2016 Republican presidential nominee displayed great energy, determination, and enthusiasm for many issues. Trump expressed outrage at the state of foreign affairs as well during his campaign.

On immigration, Trump's views rarely wavered. He wanted to build a wall around Mexico, but give it a "door" to allow in the people who would become citizens rather than remaining as illegals. Trump suggested that the Mexican government "send the bad ones over because they do not want to pay for them," in answer to a 2015 debate question about whether it was true that he thought they were sending over criminals. He also spoke about how Mexican drugs are coming into the U.S. and American money is going into Mexico.

Also, Trump said he opposed people becoming citizens solely because they were born in the United States. He also said that if he became President, he would get busy deporting illegals immediately, creating a deportation force to send illegal immigrants out of the U.S.

Another immigration issue involves what to do about ensuring terrorists don't enter the U.S. On that issue, Trump proposed banning all foreign Muslims from entering the U.S. Later, he clarified his position, saying that the ban would be temporary while the U.S. develops better means of screening out terrorists as they come into the country and that the ban would apply to countries compromised by terrorism.

On the general subject of world affairs, Trump identified himself as a deal-maker, indicating that was what was needed after the Cold War was over. He suggested that a deal-maker would put America first in all situations, even while managing many different issues at once.

In 2011, Trump wrote in *Time to Get Tough* that China would take the place of the U.S. as the largest world economy by 2027, and even sooner if things did not change. Furthermore, he stated that he "know[s] how to make America rich again," and that "China is our enemy" in this regard.

In a 2015 interview with Chuck Todd on *Meet the Press*, Trump said he would support NATO, but did not understand why America had to lead the world as its policeman. He supported fairness and rejected opposition to Russia.

During his campaign, Trump has spoken of several world leaders and how he would engage with them. He said he "would get along with Putin" as well as other world leaders who had no respect for Obama and current U.S. policies. However, he spoke out strongly against Korea's Kim Jong Un on several occasions, saying that "[China] should make him disappear."

Trump certainly did not support interfering with internal affairs in other countries. He opposed "nation-building" and indicated that the U.S. should keep its resources at home to deal with domestic issues.

With ISIS causing or claiming responsibility for terrorist attacks around the world, Trump said it was time to stop ISIS, and that it must be done quickly. He suggested sending in 20,000 to

30,000 troops to accomplish this. He said he would listen to his military advisors on the issue. For all terrorists, Trump supported waterboarding and other aggressive interrogation techniques.

Donald Trump thinks for himself on both domestic and foreign policy, as is evident by his breaks with what others in his party support or oppose. He does not care about being politically correct. In 2015, he chose to enter the race for the position of President of the U.S. to be voted on in November 2016. The Republican Party, and indeed the entire country, would never be the same again.

Chapter 15

Presidential Race 2016

On June 16, 2015, Donald Trump stood in Trump Tower in NYC and announced that he would run for President in the next election. He introduced the slogan that would carry him through the primaries and into the general election: Make America Great Again. It was only the second time in history that a person whose background was primarily in business announced they would run as a member of a major political party. And, if Trump were elected, it would be the first time for someone without any background in government positions would win. The stakes were high, but Donald Trump seemed ready for the challenge.

The Republican primaries presented voters with the largest number of choices in American history. Trump got outstanding media coverage and appealed to many voters who liked both his positions and his forthrightness in stating them. The field was narrowed down by early 2016, with only Trump and Ted Cruz still in serious contention.

Trump did exceptionally well in the primaries. By the time the Indiana primary was over, it was clear who the victor would be. RNC Chairman Reince Priebus immediately declared Trump the presumptive winner of the nomination. Trump surpassed any other candidate in the history of the Republican party with almost 14 million primary votes.

Yet, even for a man as powerful as Donald Trump, trouble can present itself unexpectedly. At one of Trump's rallies, the Secret Service stopped a British illegal from assassinating Mr. Trump.

In July, Trump's poll numbers were virtually even with Clinton's. Hers had recently dropped after the FBI pointed out her carelessness in handling important government emails.

On the campaign trail, Trump galvanized Republicans who wanted a strong and aggressive leader. He spoke blatantly about the issues, giving his own unique perspectives and criticizing those of Hillary Clinton. At times, he had dissenters removed from his rallies.

Wherever he went, he was a hit, and he was in charge.

At the 2016 Republican National Convention, Trump walked on stage to accept the nomination of the party. The music of Queen was blasting behind him as he appeared. Although there is controversy over whether he should have used that music without Queen's explicit approval, it certainly added to his commanding presence that night.

The speech was different from the speeches of other recent Republican nominees. Rather than painting a bright and optimistic future for America, Trump chose instead to remind Americans that their country was in trouble if things did not change and change fast. He outlined his political positions, highlighting his stances on immigration, terrorism and the police force. Trump criticized Hillary Clinton passionately. Then, he explained how he would make the country better. The next day, he announced Indiana Governor Mike Pence as his running mate.

Immediately following the convention, Trump's numbers went up in the polls, as is usual. However, after the Democratic Convention, Mrs.

Clinton pulled ahead. As of the first part of August, Clinton enjoyed a significant lead. However, the race was not over. November would ultimately decide the fate of Trump and of the United States.

Conclusion

Donald Trump is who he is. He is a consummate businessman and a skilled negotiator. He has the kind of intelligence it takes to graduate from Wharton and the kind of vision it takes to build monumental skyscrapers. He has strong opinions on most issues, and he does not bend to the modern social pressure to be politically correct. For these reasons and others, Trump has gained many loyal followers – and many passionate detractors.

Donald Trump will always do what is best for him. But will he do what is best for America? That is for the American voters to decide.